How will you create something beautiful together?

This interactive journal is the inspiring companion to the

award-winning "2" book, and is the perfect way to guide you and

your partner forward on your journey. If you have found love,

Turn your

you have been given life's greatest gift. Here is the place for you

life into a

to think, dream, and plan your next adventures with your loved

wonderful

one. Explore each page and answer the prompts and thought-

adventure.

provoking questions together. Carry this journal with you and fill

it with experiences you've shared, memories you've made, and

other precious writings, reminders, dreams, and aspirations.

Life was meant to be shared. It's not where you go in life, it's who you take with you that matters. It's not *what* you have in your life, but *who* you have in your life that really counts.

Love adds; it does not subtract from life. The miracle is this: Sharing life actually makes your life bigger. Love can double our joys, divide our worries, and multiply our possibilities.

Love is not about what you can take from each other; but what you can bring to each other. It's not about what you want from the other person; it's about what you wish to give the other person.

WHOSE FACE OWNS YOUR

FAVORITE SMILE?

It's often said that we can't really love anybody with whom we never laugh. Laughter and love

_____

_____

_____

_____

_____

_____

_____

_____

_____

go together like champagne and strawberries. Tell your partner what makes your heart smile!

_____

_____

_____

_____

_____

_____

_____

_____

_____

_____

_____

_____

Why observe just one anniversary a year? Why not add the day you met, or the day you first said, "I love you," or the day you got engaged? They're all great reasons to go out and celebrate.

Ticket stubs from movies, plane tickets from trips, postcards from hotels, shells from walks on he beach, dried petals from bouquets. Start a memory box today and revisit it together often.

LOVE IS THE BEST PLACE IN THE WORLD.

_____

_____

_____

_____

_____

_____

_____

_____

Plant a tree together in your yard or a nearby park. Choose one that is symbolic to you both:

_____

_____

_____

_____

_____

_____

_____

_____

_____

_____

_____

_____

An oak for solidarity; an evergreen for renewal; a red maple for passion; a cherry for affection.

A walk in the rain. A warm towel from the dryer. A candle on the table. A special toast. A dinner for two. A favorite song. A rose with breakfast in bed. The little things you do aren't little.

_____

_____

_____

_____

_____

_____

_____

_____

_____

Anticipation is the expectation of something wonderful just ahead. List 20 places you'd like to g

_____

_____

_____

_____

_____

_____

_____

_____

_____

_____

_____

_____

_____

_____

_____

_____

_____

_____

_____

_____

_____

on a date or a trip and schedule them on the calendar. Then, look forward to each one together.

_____

_____

_____

_____

_____

_____

_____

_____

_____

_____

_____

_____

_____

SAVOR
LIFE'S TINY DELIGHTS
TOGETHER.

Good friends don't always make great couples, but great couples almost always make good friends. Top secret shared by couples on their 50th anniversary: "We've always been best friends."

Cuddle up and watch romantic movies now and then. Start your list with these: *The Notebook*

Notting Hill. Pretty Woman. Legends of the Fall. Moulin Rouge. Just like Heaven. Return to Me.

Be conscious of your treasure. Never take it for granted. Find ways to honor it, care for it, strengthen and celebrate it. Now is the time to live, love, laugh, and learn all you can together.

WHEN BEING TOGETHER

IS MORE IMPORTANT

THAN WHAT YOU DO,

YOU ARE WITH

THE ONE YOU LOVE.

XOXOXOX

There are five languages of love. You can say "I love you" with your words, your touch, with thoughtful acts or gestures, with romantic presents, or by giving the gift of your time.

Every now and then go away together and leave technology behind. You'll be surprised at what you discover when you turn off your cell phones and stay somewhere with no TV or computer.

_____

_____

_____

_____

_____

_____

_____

_____

_____

Practice the art of appreciation. Make a list of things you love about your partner and share it

_____

_____

_____

_____

_____

_____

_____

_____

_____

_____

_____

_____

_____

"You're big-hearted, you're an early riser, you're a great listener, you always make me laugh."

Who
do you
LOVE?
What are
YOU
doing
about it?

A loving relationship isn't the history channel. Let go of simple, daily annoyances. Make a list of old, small disappointments. Then throw the list away to signify you're moving forward.

_____

_____

_____

_____

_____

_____

_____

_____

_____

Music and romance go together. Do you have a favorite love song? If not, pick one ou

_____

_____

_____

_____

_____

_____

_____

_____

_____

_____

_____

_____

_____

together. Dance to it in your living room or play it as you fall asleep in each other's arms.

First bicycle, first job, first date, first kiss. Life's "firsts" fade away; you have to replace them

_____

_____

_____

_____

_____

_____

_____

with new ones. When is the next time you and your partner will do something for the first time?

_____

_____

_____

_____

_____

_____

_____

_____

_____

_____

LIFE IS A SHARED EXPERIENCE.

Everyone appreciates being appreciated. Appreciation is simply taking the time to tell your partner exactly what you like about him or her. (How do I love thee? Let me count the ways.)

It's human nature to talk about our dislikes with the person closest to us. Your partner is

_____

_____

_____

_____

_____

_____

_____

_____

_____

probably already aware of all the things you *don't* like. Now make a list of what you *do* like.

_____

_____

_____

_____

_____

_____

_____

_____

_____

_____

_____

When you count your blessings, count your problems too. Problems test, polish, and unite us

Troubles are a natural part of life—and sometimes the *best* part, if you face them together.

TEXT LESS & CALL MORE.

What good is love if it's not expressed? If you love someone, be sure to find ways to show it

It's not how much we love and appreciate someone that's important, it's how much they know it.

Looking at old pictures together. Take turns recalling who you were when each photo was

_____

_____

_____

_____

_____

_____

_____

_____

_____

taken. Share the ways your hopes, dreams, and perspectives have changed through the years.

_____

_____

_____

_____

_____

_____

_____

_____

_____

_____

_____

It's good to remember that the most dangerous threat to couples is not money, compatibility, or even fidelity. The most dangerous threat is, by far, simply taking each other for granted.

When it matters,

don't

wait.

Wishes granted here! Try exchanging wish lists with each other: "I wish we would adopt a dog together. I wish you would gift wrap your presents. I wish you wouldn't work on weekends."

It's simple: love is good for you. A healthy, loving relationship can lower blood pressure, ease stress, raise self-esteem, stimulate creativity, increase focus, fight off aging, and extend life.

As children we are taught that one plus one is two. But when the right people come together, one plus one is more than two. Together you are able to do what neither of you could do alone.

Use this interactive journal on its own or with the companion book, 2: How will you create something beautiful together?

Discover all of the Life by the Numbers books and journals!

1: How many people does it take to make a difference?

5: Where will you be five years from today?

7: How many days of the week can be extraordinary?

10: What's on your top 10 list?